AN EARFULL OF DESIGNS

by
Sigrid Wynne-Evans

Computer Illustrations
by Lori Berry

Copyright MCMXCV by Sigrid Wynne-Evans

All rights reserved. No part of this book may be reproduced or transmitted in any form or by any means, electronic or mechanical, including but not restricted to, photocopying, recording or by any information storage and/or retrieval system without prior permission in writing from the author.

These designs are intended for personal use only. Mass marketing of the designs as finished work or as kits is prohibited without written permission from the author.

Sigrid Wynne-Evans

The Beaded Bear
P.O. Box 110894
Campbell, CA 95011

Wynne-Evans, Sigrid, 1956-

    An Earfull of Designs/by Sigrid Wynne-Evans
    p. cm.
    ISBN # 0-9648360-0-9

CREDITS

Publishing your own book for the first time is a learning experience. Such an endeavor could not have been done without a lot of help from some very good friends. Here is my heartfelt thanks to all those who supported me and cheered me through every step of the process.

Nancy Donnelley— who many years ago encouraged my design process.

Linda Benmour — who always said "you *can* do it!"

Eagle's View Publishing — who got me out there.

Ralph Allen — who had the patience to do my photography, and gave me more ideas than I could ever handle.

Lori Berry — what would I have done without your encouragement -- and computer skills?

Eileen Bonomo of Griffin Printing — who walked me through the printing process.

My best friend and daughter, **Jasmine**, who can always make me laugh in the oddest situations.

And of course thanks to all my fans who've written, and called crying "where is your book?"

And finally — a *big raspberry* to those of you who doubted.

Dear Beaders:

Well finally, here is another book of patterns!!! I hope that you will enjoy this book as much as you have enjoyed my other books. I would like to thank all of you who have written and called to give me the encouragement to write another book. I could not have done it without all your support!!!

It is quite a thrill for me to see my designs crafted by other beaders. I have seen my designs pop up at many Craft Fairs and as well in another book (which gave me the credit as the designer). What gives me a special delight is to see how you have taken the basic design and added your own special touches. Some of what I've seen I have never even considered doing. So you are even giving me ideas. Keep up the great work!!!!

I welcome any comments and suggestions that you may have. I try to answer all letters (please send a SASE for reply). Who knows, perhaps there will be another book in the works!!??!!

BLISSFUL BEADING!!

SIG

TABLE OF CONTENTS

The Basics 1

The Craft Business 6

Directions 8

Designs 14

    Beginner Designs 14

    Alaska/Whale 15

    Bikini Girl 16

    Donkey 17

    Eagle Kachina Dancer 18

    Egret 19

    Eye of Horus 20

    Fire Serpent 21

    Fox 22

    Fushias 23

    Geraniums 24

    Happy Moon 25

    Holding the Moon 26

    Hot Air Balloon 27

    Hummingbird 28

    Hyacinth Macaw 29

    In 30

    Japanese Crane 31

    Kabuki Mask 32

    Kool Kat 33

Marilyn #1 34
Marilyn #2 35
Mime 36
Out 37
Peony 38
Pheasant 39
Poppy 40
Rainbow and Pot o' Gold 41
Rainbow Steed 42
Rearinghorse 43
Red Tail Hawk 44
Rockhopper Penguin 45
Scottie 46
Sheep 47
Shepherdess 48
Tiger 49
Turtle #1 50
Turtle #2 51
Wolf 52
Woodpecker 53
Yin-Yang 54

BLANK GRAPHS FOR YOUR OWN DESIGNS 55

Triangle 55
Diamond 56

THE BASICS

There are few materials needed to create the earrings in this book. In fact, you can buy supplies to make a pair of earrings for less than the cost of this book. The choices of beads and beading supplies that are available are vast. The correct choices will make the earrings beautiful, while the wrong choices may make the earrings less than appealing. Therefore, I will attempt to give you a bead primer in hopes that your choices will help you make a spectacular pair of earrings.

NEEDLE AND THREAD

The easiest choices that you will have will be the type of needle and thread that you will use. Most of you will choose to use a size 11^0 bead (more about bead sizes later). For this size bead, a size 12 beading needle will do just fine.

Beading needles differ from regular sewing needles in that they are longer and thinner. The eye is narrow and long as compared to a sewing needle. This is an important feature in that the holes in beads are fairly small and you will be passing the needle and thread through the bead more than once.

Beading needles are available in several sizes. Size 12 is the most commonly used. A size 15 needle will be needed for size 14 beads. As with beads, the higher the number, the smaller the diameter of the needle.

"NYMO" beading thread is highly recommended for any type of seed bead work. Do not use regular sewing thread as it has a tendency to fray much too quickly. "NYMO" thread is a nylon thread which is fairly strong and is available in several sizes. My personal preference is to use size O or A. Other beaders like to use size B, which is thicker. Since some Czech beads have quite small holes, even in size 11^0 beads, the B thread may fill up the beads in the base row so that you will not be able to pass through the beads for the completion of the fringe. Therefore, I use the smaller size thread to ensure that I will be able to pass through the bead several times.

Many beaders like to wax the thread with bee's wax. The wax will help keep the thread from fraying and knotting. I do not wax my thread. Again, this is just a personal preference. I do not like the waxy feel of the thread. Sometimes the wax also builds up on the top of the beads. The wax also adds bulk to the thread which may be just enough to fill up the hole of the bead so that you won't be able to pass through the required amount of times.

While I have given you my own personal preferences as a starting point for your choices of needle and thread, I do not mean to imply that other choices are wrong. Try other choices to see if they work better for you. There really is no single right way, only what works best for you. So experiment!

BEADS, BEADS, AND MORE BEADS

Now, we have reached the fun part!! And also the most difficult in terms of the choices that you will have available to you.

Seed Beads are the basis for the designs in this book. Bugle beads and the small 4mm crystals may be used at the end of the dangles as accents. There is a wide array of seed beads available. A basic knowledge of the different types and styles that are available will help you with your selection of beads for the earrings in this book.

Seed beads are packaged for sale in many different ways. Some stores will package beads in small tubes, others will sell them by the hank. On occasion you will also see seed beads packaged by weight. How these beads are sold often depends on how the supplier distributes the beads. So, if you are comparing prices, about the only fair way to compare price is to know the price per kilo or per gram.

Seed beads come in different sizes, the most common sizes are 9^0, 10^0, 11^0, 12^0, 13^0, 14^0, 15^0 and 16^0. Of these, 11^0 is the most widely used. Remember, the higher the number, the smaller the bead.

When working the designs in this book, bead size uniformity is very important. Beads will vary in size within a hank and from manufacturer to manufacturer. I've used 11^0 beads that look more like 10^0, and 11^0 beads that look more like 12^0. Care must be taken in choosing beads!

Size 11^0 will work well for the designs in this book. It does make for a rather large showy earring. If you are a beginner, then I would recommend that you start by using size 11^0, simply because you will have more to hold on to. If you prefer a smaller earring, then try size 14^0 bead. Using size 14^0 is really not any more difficult and you will have a significantly smaller earring.

The number one rule of buying beads is to buy all the beads you will need (or can possibly buy) of the style/color that you intend to use. If you favor certain colors, it may be in your best interest to buy bulk (1/4 kilo or more) because unless you are very organized and lucky, you will either forget where you bought those beads, or the dye lot has changed, or the worst of all possibilities — it is a discontinued color/style. This has happened to me several times. Also, the bead import business or the reliability of the manufacturer may be such that your favorite store is out of that particular bead and it may take 6 months for them to get another shipment.

This has happened to me with a particular Japanese bead that I liked. I called the bead store every 2-3 weeks for 5 months before they were restocked. I now have a good sized jar **full**!! I won't run out for quite a while. Incidentally, that bead store was out of that bead **again** 6 weeks after I bought my stock!

So, enough about size and on to style.

Seed beads can come in a variety of cuts. Smooth beads have been tumbled to give their surface a regular texture. There are no facets. These are probably what you think of as the typical bead.

Cut seed beads can be found as 2-cuts, 3-cuts, and hex-cuts, with facets on 2, 3, and 6 sides respectively.

Charlotte beads have little facets cut into them on 1 or 2 sides. These beads reflect the light very nicely and can give your piece a very elegant look.

Seed beads also come in a variety of finishes. The most common ones are listed below:

Aurora Borealis (AB), also known as **Iris**, **Iridescent**, or **Fire Polish**: These have a rainbow effect on the surface.

Ceylon: Surface is some what pearlized.

Delica: A new bead which has become very popular. These beads are laser cut, and are extremely uniform in size. They are pricey, but since they are nearly all usable the price is well worth it. Do not mix these beads with the regular seed beads, since they are sized differently.

Greasy: This is an "old" finish. It's opaque, but has depth. The colors are very limited. Yellow, turquoise, and green are the most common.

Matte: A dull finish (with no shine). These beads are the current rage.

Opaque: Light will not pass through these beads. Sometimes these are referred to as chalky colors.

Transparent: Light passes through these beads, giving your piece a stained glass appearance.

Beads To Beware Of!!!!

Metallic beads look so beautiful. They shine so beautifully and are spectacular in a piece. But alas, how they fade!!

I've used some metallic Czechoslovakian beads in a beautiful fuchsia and a brilliant blue. The earrings were spectacular! But two days in the sun made them fade from those lovely colors to wishy washy colors with strong tin color overtones. In short, a disgusting color that no one would like.

Japan is manufacturing some lovely metallics that I've been seduced by. Before I use them in a major project, I'll test them by leaving them out in the sun and by washing them to see how they hold up. Rumor amongst those in the know is that they do last provided that you don't shower with them or use them in areas where perspiration and body oils will degrade them.

Surface dyed beads are another problem bead. If they aren't marked as such, the give away signs are: a mottled appearance on the surface of the bead (uneven color) or the holes will have a tendency to be a tad darker than the surface. I've had some poor quality beads that were pretty enough in their package, but the color rubbed off during the course of working with the piece! Pinks are especially prone to this. So keep your eyes open to this problem.

Color lined beads (also known as "inside color") may also be a problem. These beads have a different color painted in the hole from what the outside color is. Sometimes this inside color can rub off.

Choosing Colors

I have provided a color code for each design in this book. The color codes are only a suggestion or a guide. These colors have worked well for me, but if you wish, try other colors.

From the above discussion on beads, you can see that if the code calls for a "RED" bead, you will still have to choose what type of "RED" bead to use. The choice of color and type of finish of the bead can make or break the design. With the simpler designs, involving 2-3 colors, the choice of beads may not be as critical. Beads with a reasonable contrast will almost always work. However, on complex designs involving 5 or more colors, particularly when 2 or more shades of the same color are used, contrast will become critical.

One of the first lessons in creating designs that are identifiable is that if several colors of transparent beads are used together, they tend to blend in together. For example, light pink with white or pink with lavender. Since the success of the design will depend heavily on the distinction of color changes, you will not want a blending of colors.

When choosing colors, generally I will choose colors that are as distinct as I can possibly find. If you choose your colors by laying hanks of beads together, you may be surprised to find that even if the hanks contrast well, if you were to place one or two beads of each color together, they may be nearly indistinguishable. Always put one or two beads of each color together on a needle if there is any question of whether or not the beads will hold their own distinct color or if the eye will blend them together. This is especially important for transparent beads, although some opaque hues may need this test as well.

Transparent beads are wonderful for background colors, especially if opaque colors are used for the design. Light will pass through the transparent beads making them recess into the background, while the light will stop or reflect back to the eye on the opaque beads used in the design. This type of contrast is strong.

Areas requiring a strong definition such as outlines should almost always be done in opaque beads.

AN EXTRA TIP

Uniformity of bead size will always be important. When the design continues into the dangle of the earring, uniformity is critical. When looking at a hank of beads, you will notice that there is some variation in size. Some may be fat while others may be slivers. Try to choose beads that are fairly uniform. There may be on occasion, when the beads you've chosen seem fairly uniform, but the line or continuity of the design is not as you would like it to be. Add or subtract a bead as needed to achieve the desired effect. Horizontal lines near the middle and ends of the dangles are prone to this adjustment. With each dangle that you string, always check the alignment and the continuity of the design and make the modifications as needed. If the pattern calls for 10 black beads on a strand and 9 beads will keep the horizontal line straight, make that adjustment. It is more important to maintain the design continuity than it is to keep the exact number of beads that the graph calls for.

THE CRAFT BUSINESS

One day many of you will want to venture into business selling your beadwork. When I first began, I had no idea of how to go about selling my beadwork. It took years of research and many hard knocks to learn what I know now. I will give you a few ideas on getting started so that your start won't be as much as a struggle as mine was.

There are several ways in which to sell your beadwork. The most common ways are: 1.) direct sales, such as wholesale and retail; and 2.) consignment. Each of these has endless possibilities.

When you are first starting out, consignment is probably the first opportunity that will come your way. Consignment means that the store will keep your merchandise and will pay you a percentage of the selling price after the piece has sold. Most seasoned craftspeople will not take on consignment accounts because there are some very definite drawbacks. But for the beginner, a consignment account may be a very good opportunity to sell beadwork provided that certain pitfalls are avoided. The main thing that I want to impress upon you is that the store has no risk in consignments. So if you agree to consignments, be sure that YOU set the terms, because if anyone loses it will be you.

Consignment agreements will vary from store to store. Consignment agreements may be 70/30, 60/40, or 50/50. The first number is the percentage of the sale that you will get, the second number is the percentage of the selling price that the store will retain. Be sure to find out if the store will add on their commission to your asking price or if they will subtract their commission from your price. Depending on the answer, you may have to adjust your prices accordingly.

With consignment accounts be sure that you get all the specifics in writing. Have everything spelled out such as: when you will be paid (after each sale or monthly), who is responsible for theft or damage (don't sign the agreement if the store assumes no such liability), what percent of the selling price you are to receive, and how much of a notice will be required of you to pick up your work if you wish to reclaim possession.

Another way to sell beadwork, and in my opinion, a more fun and profitable way, is at Art and Craft Shows. There is a significant investment required before you can participate in a show as you will need to acquire an acceptable display, i.e., canopy, tables and possibly a display case. In addition, some show fees are expensive. The advantage in participating in the shows is that you are selling at retail cost rather than at wholesale, and the potential for repeat business as well as custom work is high. Also, you may get calls for your work from someone who picked up your card long after the show is over.

Before participating in a show, visit the event to try to get a feel for how well attended it is and try to get an idea if your work would be well received with the clientele. If you're lucky enough to find a beader at the show, try to see if she (he) is willing to share some information with you. While some people are rather tight lipped about the whole process, others are more than willing to try to help.

A word on pricing — a general formula used by many crafters is: Wholesale Price = cost of materials x 3 + hourly wage. While this is a guide, it is not the end all in pricing. Most people forget to consider costs such as gas and time to go to stores to buy supplies, storage equipment, packaging or cards for displays and many other incidental costs. With all things considered, a pair of seed bead earrings may only cost at most $5 to make, perhaps the most important consideration is the time involved.

I am a rather vocal advocate of beaders getting paid for their artistry. Few of us actually do. Yet there are some beaders who give away their work. This is what angers me. I've seen some beaders who've made my designs and sold them for about $22. I know the time involved. DO NOT SELL THEM SO CHEAPLY!!! My wholesale prices for most of my earrings range from $32-$40 depending on the complexity and the type of beads and accents used. My retail prices range from about $45-$65 on most earrings. If the store tells you that you are too expensive, then you have not found the right market for your work. Keep looking!!! Those of you who sell too cheaply do a great disservice to the rest of us, and reinforce the idea that beadwork is a "CHEAP" form of art.

DIRECTIONS

The earrings in this book are of two types, the diamond and the triangle. Both are done using the Comanche Weave. This weave is also called the Brick Stitch, Bedouin Stitch, Apache Weave and probably several other names. If you have never done the Comanche Weave before, I strongly suggest that you practice the base row using bugles until you feel very comfortable with the technique. These earrings require that the base row be done with seed beads. There is no difference in the technique, but it does take an understanding of what the tension needs to be as well as a good deal of dexterity in the fingertips. It is much easier to learn how to do the base row with bugles and you will become much less frustrated.

These earrings are done in three parts — the base row, top, and dangles. We begin with the base row, which is the widest row of the earring. I start off with about an arm's length of thread. Whether or not you wax the thread with bee's wax is up to you. It can help keep the thread from tangling and fraying, but it can also add bulk to the thread and give a waxy buildup on the tops of the beads.

If you are a beginner, please try both of the beginner patterns before trying the larger, more complicated designs.

STEP 1: BASE ROW

Pick up two beads and slide them down towards the end of the thread (I like to leave about a 6 inch tail for finishing). Then go **up** through the first bead only and pull tight. This will bring the beads side by side.

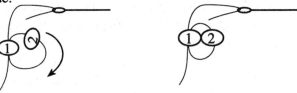

Now go **down** through the second bead. This should leave the beads looking like this:

With your thumb and index finger, hold these two beads closely together and make sure that the thread is tight! Pick up one bead and go **down** through bead number 2 and pull tight. Notice how you are following the direction of the thread? Think of making full circles, with the needle and thread. You now have 3 beads side by side with your thread coming out of the bottom of the second bead.

Before you can pick up another bead, you must always have the thread coming out of the last bead. So now go **up** through that 3rd bead.

Now you can pick up another bead. Bring the needle and thread once again **up** through that last bead and pull tight. Remember, think of making a full circle whenever you add a new bead!

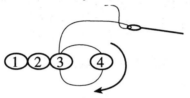

Bring the needle and thread **down** through the last bead.

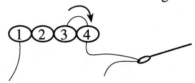

Hopefully, you are seeing a pattern emerging. Your needle and thread are following a circular motion. Always follow the direction of the thread. Continue in this manner until you have the required number of beads for the base row.

STEP 2: BODY

If you have an odd number of beads in the base row, you will see that the needle and thread is coming out of the top of the last bead. If the base row has an even number, then flip the beads over so that the thread is coming out of the top of the last bead.

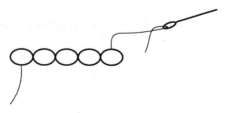

Again, you will be adding one bead at a time. Pick up a bead. Bring the needle and thread (from back to front) under the threads connecting the two beads in the base row. Then bring the needle and thread up through that bead. Pull tight. Continue in this manner until you have just two beads in a row. You will be weaving right to left, then the next row will be left to right. Each row will decrease by one bead. Note: threads are shown loose for clarity of illustration. Your threads should be tight.

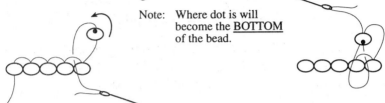

Note: Where dot is will become the <u>BOTTOM</u> of the bead.

STEP 3: EARRING LOOP

Once you have two beads on the top, it is time to make the earring loop. Pick up 6 beads along with the earring wire. Go down through the adjacent bead. Go around this loop at least 2 more times to give strength to this area of high wear.

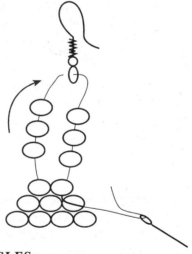

STEP 4: DANGLES

Work the needle and thread down through the top portion until you come out of the end base row bead. If you are making one of the triangle designs, turn the work upside down and do the work as you did on the top (except for the earring loop). This will give you the diamond shape.

Dangles for the triangle shaped earrings are easy. Read the chart vertically. Put on all the beads in the vertical row along with any accent beads such as bugles and/or crystals that you wish. DARE to get crazy!! Once you have them all on, then go back up through the beads again, as well as the base row bead that you came out of. You must leave at least one bead to hold all those beads in place. If you put 3 beads as the anchors, you will have a nice little "flower".

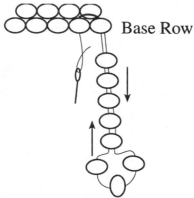

Base Row

For the diamond earrings, there are two ways to add dangles. One is to add dangles in the same manner as with the triangle. Note that a dangle will come out of every other row. The other way is to make loops. Note that one side of the loop will be one bead longer to compensate for the uneven placement of the loop.

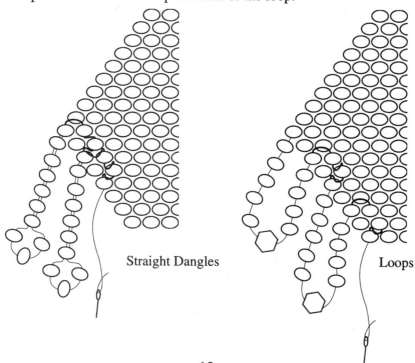

Straight Dangles   Loops

Another way is to make loops. Again, you will be going into every other row. Note that the portion of the loop that is on the lower row will have two beads less. This is to compensate for the shorter distance traveled.

STEP 5: FINISHING/ADDING NEW THREAD

To finish old thread, weave the thread up and down several beads in the body of the work. If you wish, a small knot can be tied on the edge of the beadwork, much as you would if you were hand sewing. Although it is harder to do, a knot is better hidden if you can place it in between beads of the body.

Add new thread by tying a knot on the edge, then weave the thread to where you left off.

To finish the earring, bring the needle and thread out of the top portion of the earring. A simple knot on the edge of the earring will end your work. I like to take a match and melt the nymo after the knot has been made. Care must be taken so that you don't melt other threads. The advantage of melting the thread is that it helps to keep the end from pulling through as it adheres onto itself. Adding thread is done in the same manner. If the white nymo shows too much on the edges, use a felt tipped pen to color the thread.

Hopefully, you will master this technique with few problems. These designs will give you a lot of fun as well as a good challenge. They are a departure from the traditional geometric designs. I have tried to incorporate good color sense as well as some humor. I hope you will enjoy these designs as much as I do. I would enjoy hearing how you like the designs and if you would like to see more design books. If you write, be sure to include a SASE for reply.

Beginner Design #1
With Bugle Bead Base Row

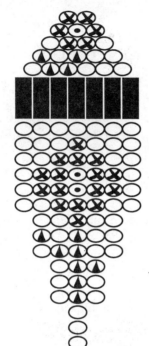

Beginner Design #2
With Seed Bead Base Row

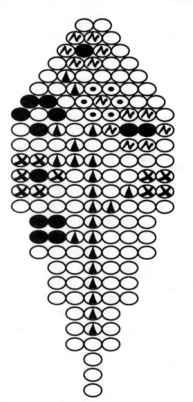

✗   Red

▲   Green

•   Yellow

●   Purple

∾   Orange

○   White

Alaska/Whale

- •   Sky Blue
- ◯   White
- ✕   Green
- —   Dk. Green
- ∼   Blue
- ●   Black-Grey

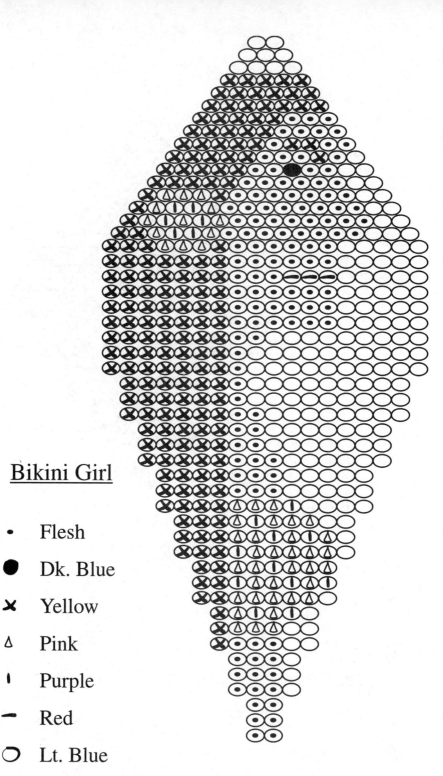

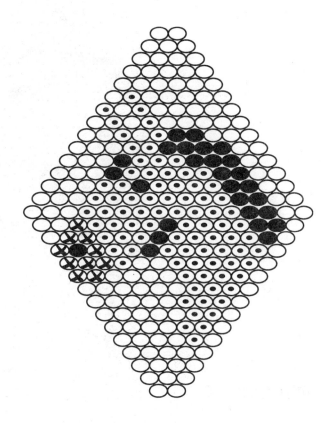

Donkey

- • Grey
- ● Black
- ✕ Tan
- ○ White

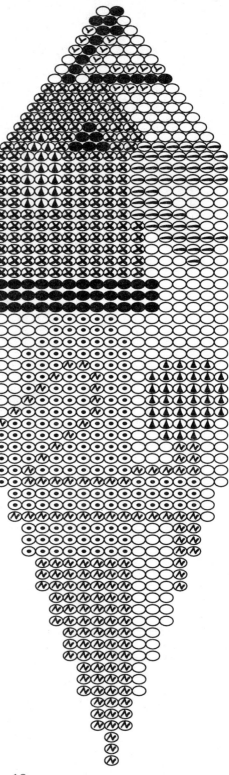

Eagle
Kachina Dancer

- ✖ Green
- ▲ Red
- — Orange
- • Tan
- ∼ Brown
- ● Black
- ˅ White
- ○ Cream

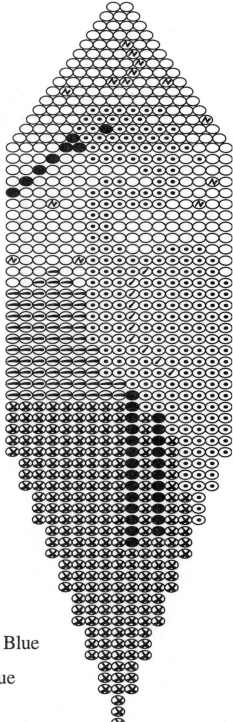

Egret

- •   White
- ●   Black
- —   Green
- ∿   Yellow
- ○   Dk. Transparent Blue
- ✖   Silver Lined Blue
- ╱   Grey

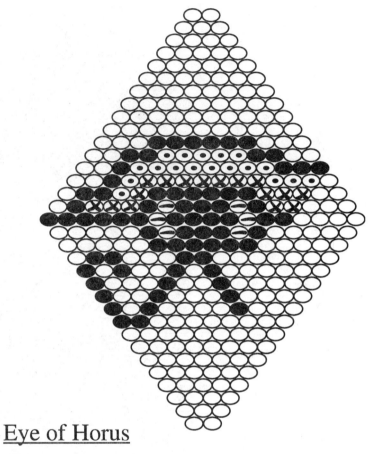

Eye of Horus

- ● Black
- — White
- • Blue
- ✗ Red
- ○ Gold Irridescent

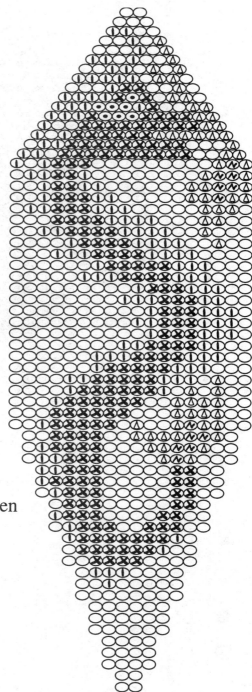

Fire Serpent

✖ Metallic Green
△ Red
∿ Orange
| Gold
• Pink
○ Background

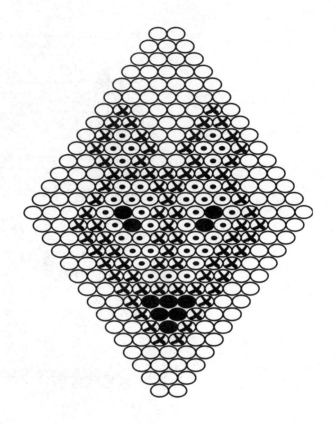

Fox

✘ Rust

• White

● Black

○ Green

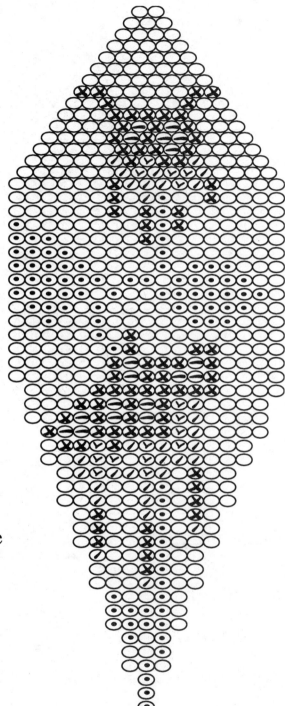

Fushias

— Lt. Purple

✗ Purple

╱ Pink

ᴠ Lt. Pink

• Green

○ Background

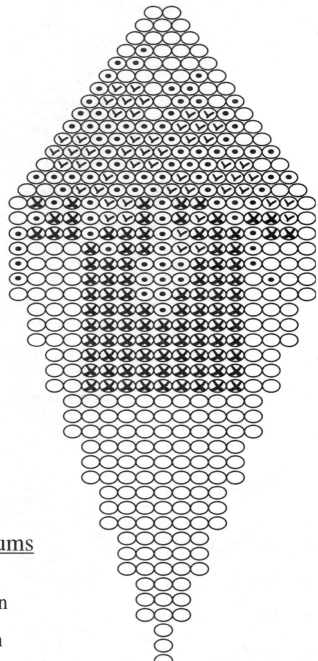

Geraniums

✘ Brown

• Green

✔ Red

◯ Background

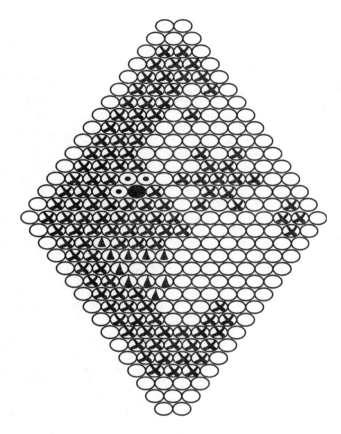

Happy Moon

✘   Silver Lined Yellow

●   Black

▲   Red

•   White

◯   Dk. Blue

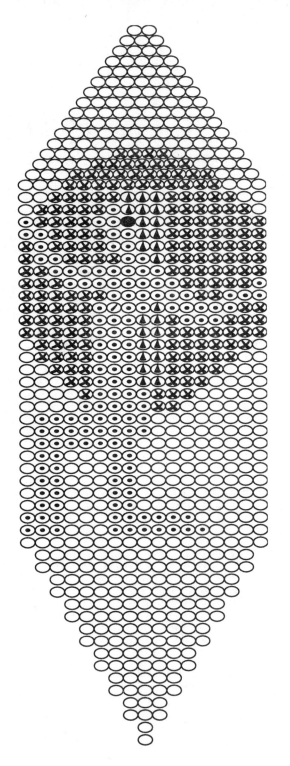

Holding the Moon

✖ Silver

• Flesh

╱ Rose

● Blue

▲ Brown

○ Violet

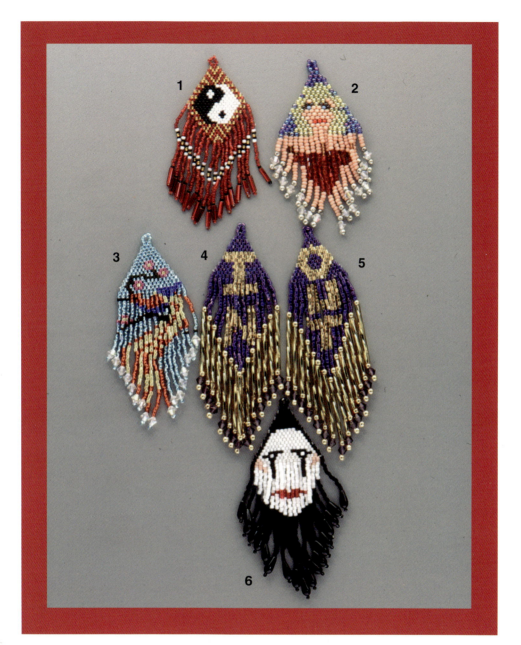

1. Yin-Yang

2. Marilyn #1

3. Pheasant

4. In (one ear)

5. Out (the other)

6. Mime

1. Hyacinth Macaw
2. Eye of Horus
3. Donkey
4. Kabuki Mask
5. Bikini Girl
6. Fox

1. Woodpecker
2. Rearing Horse
3. Holding the Moon
4. Peony
5. Rainbow Steed
6. Tiger

1. Eagle Kachina Dancer
2. Happy Moon
3. Red Tail Hawk
4. Alaska/Whale
5. Hot Air Balloon

1. Shepherdess

2. Sheep

3. Fushia

4. Turtle #2

5. Geraniums

6. Rainbow & Pot of Gold

1. Rockhopper Penguin
2. Turtle #1
3. Marilyn #2
4. Kool Kat
5. Wolf
6. Terrier

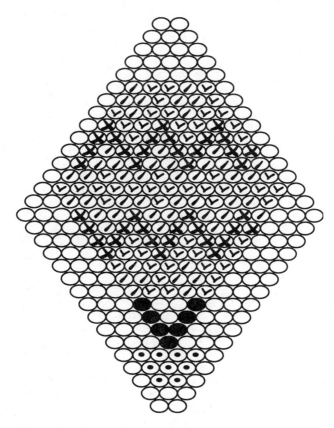

Hot Air Balloon

- ✖ Yellow
- ● Black
- · Brown
- ⌄ Blue
- ╱ Pink
- ◯ Sky Blue

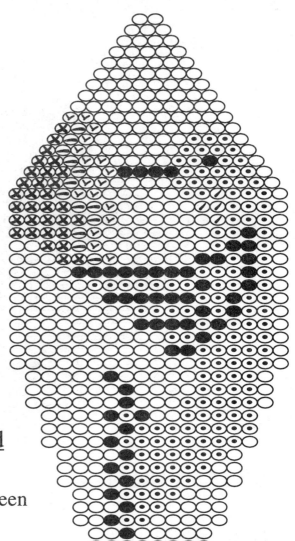

Hummingbird

- •   Irridescent Green
- ✗   Purple
- —   White
- ˅   Pink
- ●   Black
- ╱   Irridescent Fushia
- ○   Background

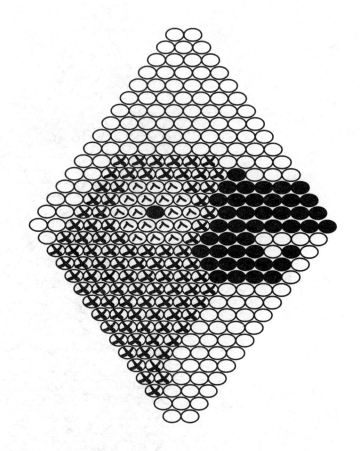

Hyacinth Macaw

- ︿ Dk. Blue
- ● Black
- ✘ Yellow
- ◯ White

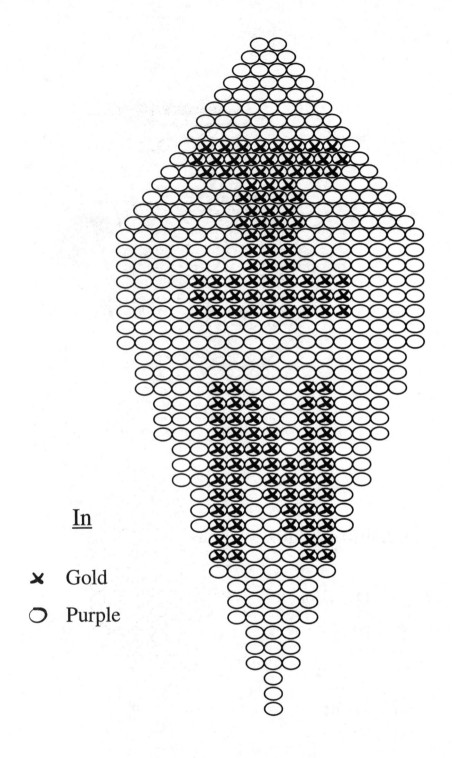

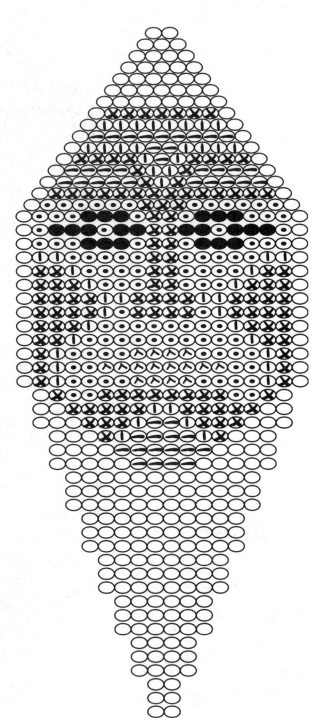

Kabuki Mask

- ✘ Dk. Blue
- | Gold
- — Pink
- • White
- ● Black
- ʌ Red
- ○ Crystal

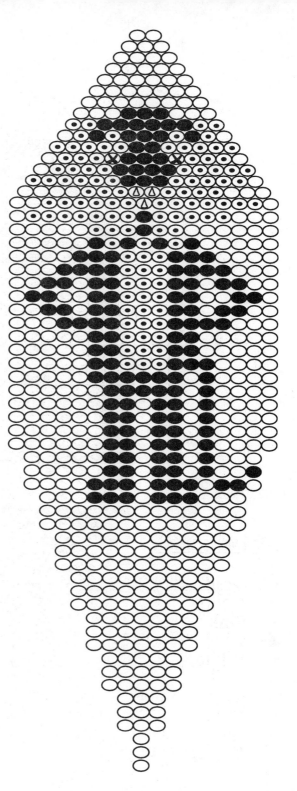

Kool Kat

- • White
- ● Black
- △ Pink
- ✕ Green
- ○ Hot Pink

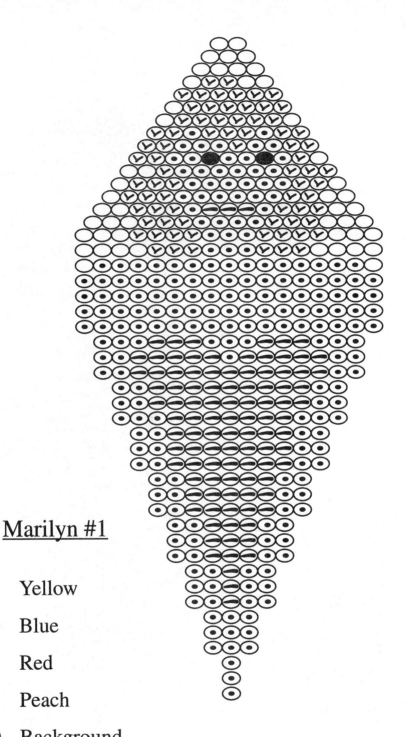

Marilyn #1

- ⌄ Yellow
- ● Blue
- — Red
- · Peach
- ○ Background

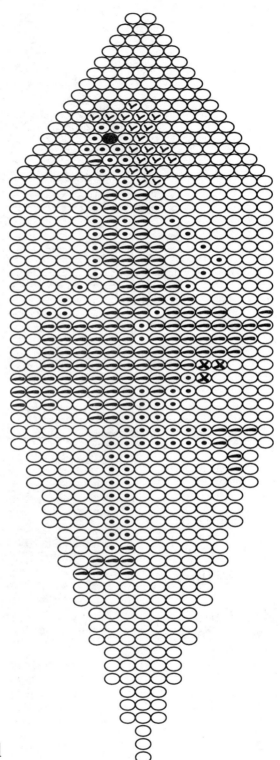

Marilyn #2

- • Peach
- ᵛ Yellow
- ● Blue
- — Red
- ✗ Black
- ○ Background

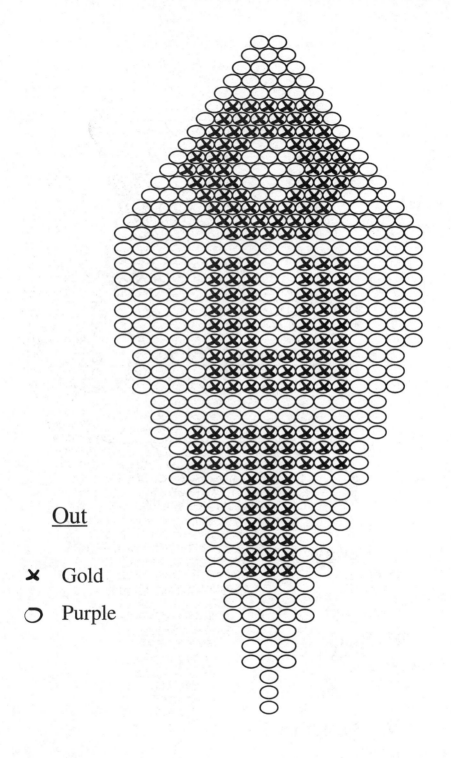

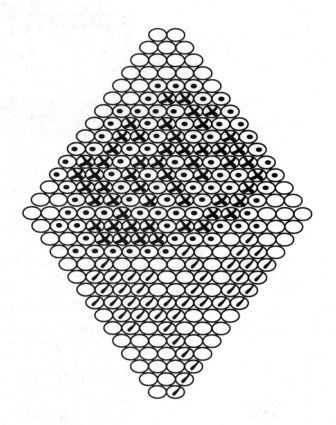

Peony

✗   Gold

•   Pink

╱   Green

◯   Background

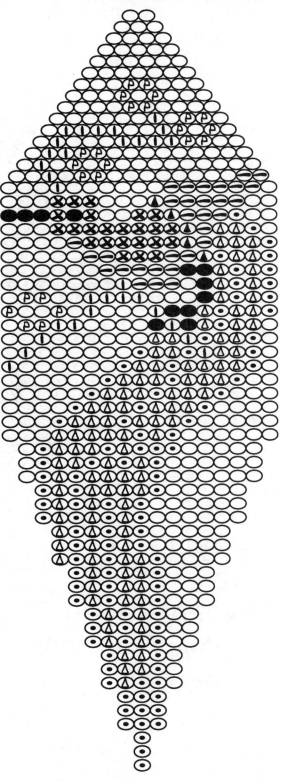

Pheasant

∣	Brown
●	Black
₽	Pink
✕	Red
∆	Yellow
•	Orange
▲	Blue
—	Green
⬭	Light Blue

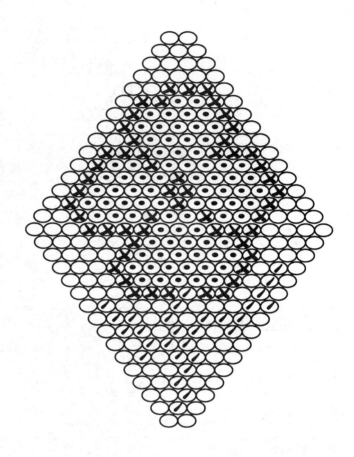

Poppy

✗ Black
• Orange
╱ Green
◯ Blue

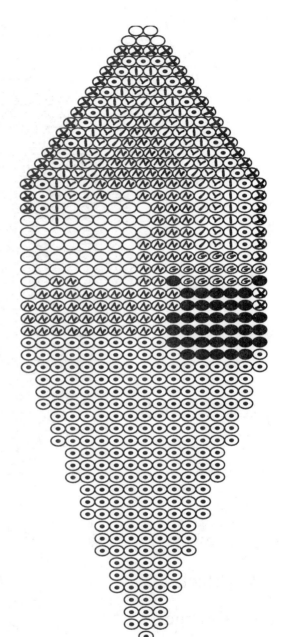

Rainbow and Pot o' Gold

- ɞ Gold
- ⌵ Orange
- ╱ Red
- • Green
- ✕ Blue
- ● Black
- ○ White
- ∾ Sky Blue
- ∣ Yellow

41

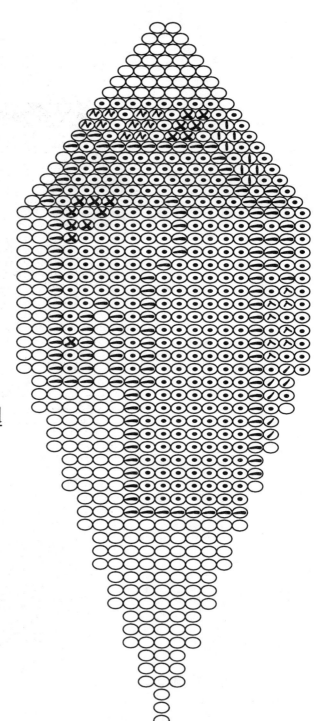

Rainbow Steed

- ⋏ Purple
- ✘ Red
- — Yellow
- ⋀ Green
- ╱ Blue
- • Black
- ǀ Orange
- ⌒ Background

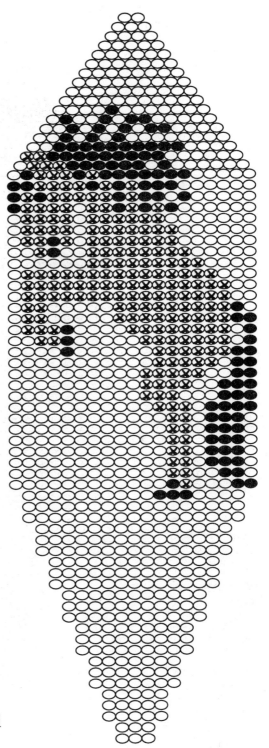

Rearinghorse

- ● Black
- ✘ Brown
- ○ Background

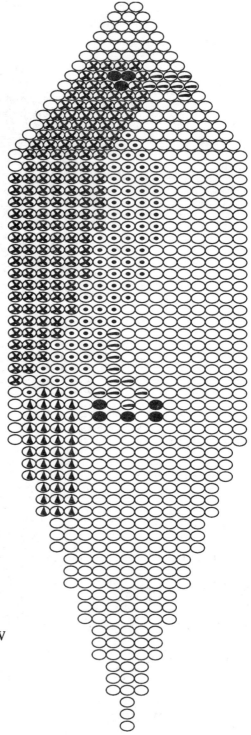

Red Tail Hawk

- ✖ Brown
- • Tan
- ● Black
- ━ Orange/Yellow
- ▲ Rust
- ○ Background

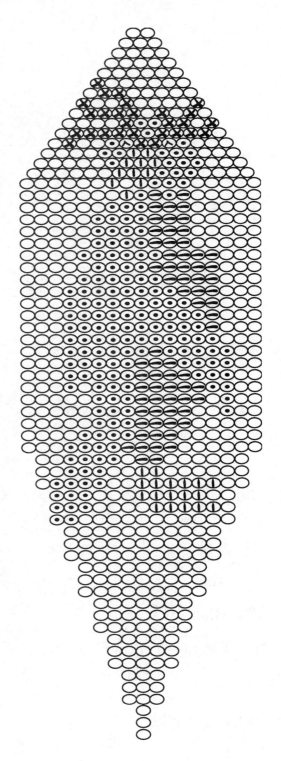

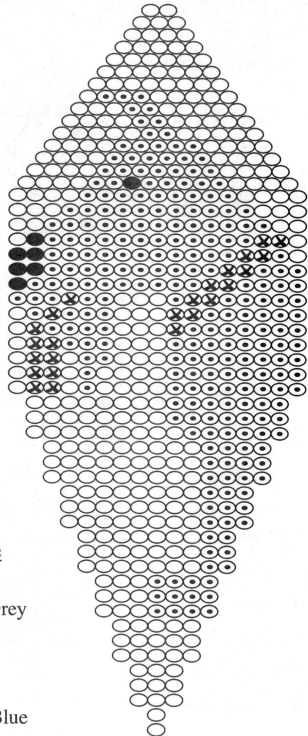

Scottie

- Dark Grey
- Black
- Red
- Light Blue

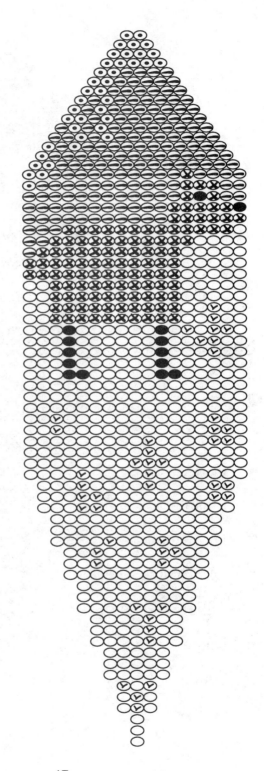

Sheep

- ● Black
- · Sky Blue
- ✗ White
- — Rust
- ○ Sand
- ✓ Green

Shepherdess

- ● Black
- • Sky Blue
- ✕ Red
- + Flesh
- ∿ Dk. Blue
- ╱ Dk. Brown
- ⇌ Silver
- — Rust
- ○ Sand
- ⌄ Green

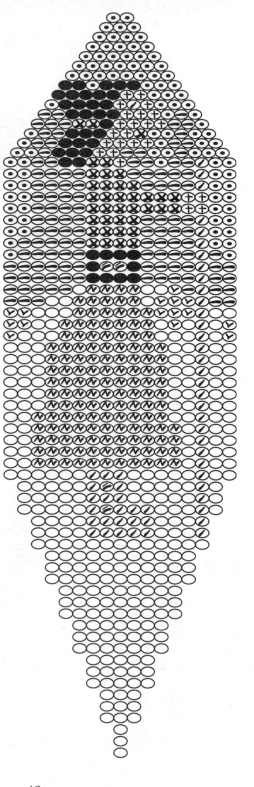

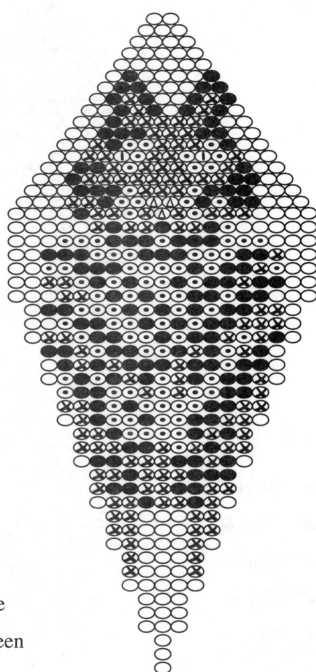

Tiger

- ● Black
- · White
- ✕ Orange
- ı Lt. Green
- ○ Green
- △ Pink

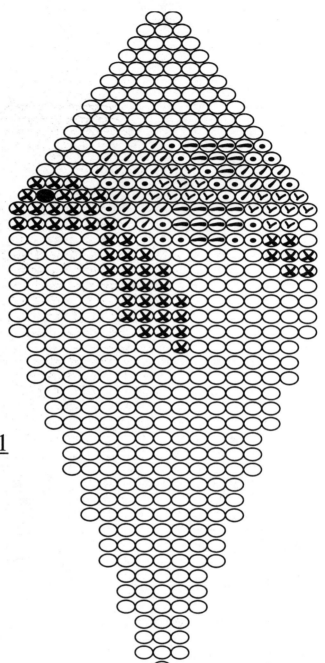

Turtle #1

- ● Black
- ✖ Orange
- ╱ Blue
- • Yellow
- ⋎ Pink
- ─ Green
- ○ Background

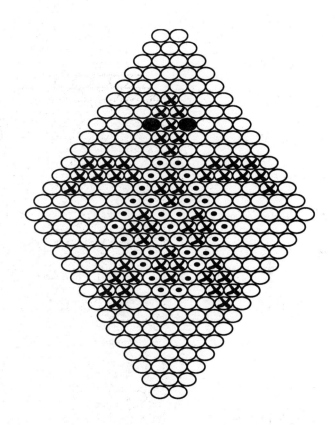

Turtle #2

✘ Green

• Dk. Green

● Yellow

○ Bronze

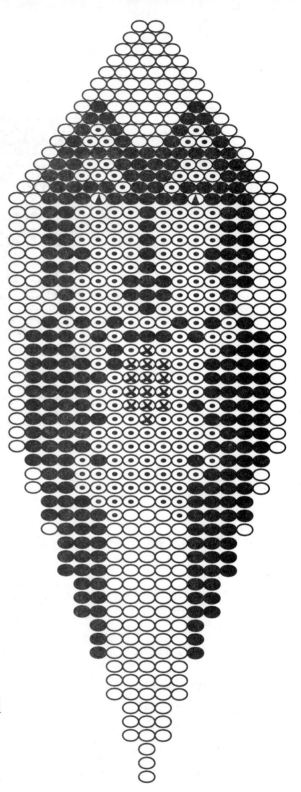

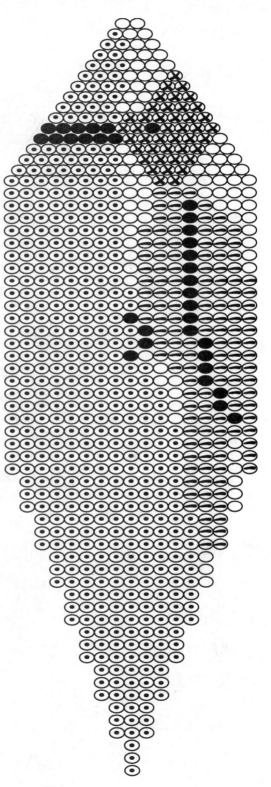

Woodpecker

- •   Dark Brown
- ●   Black
- ✗   Red
- —   Light Brown
- ○   Blue

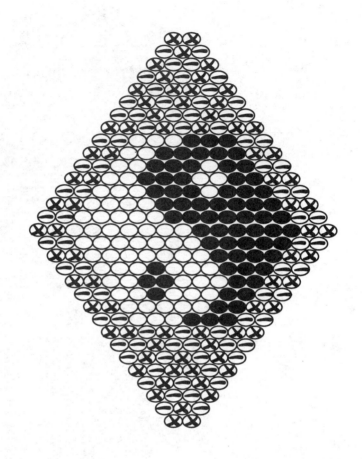

Yin-Yang

- ○ White
- ● Black
- ✕ Red
- ─ Orange

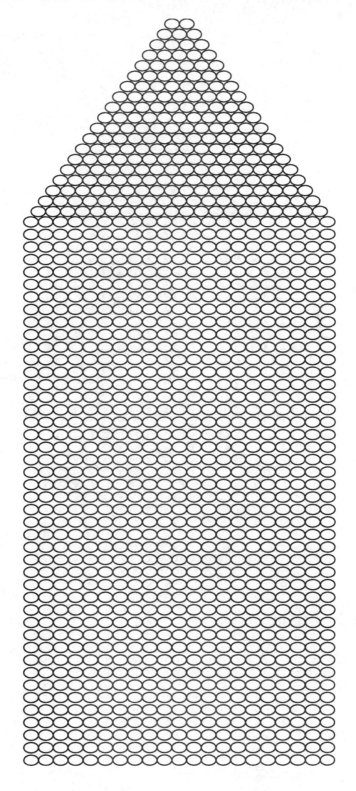

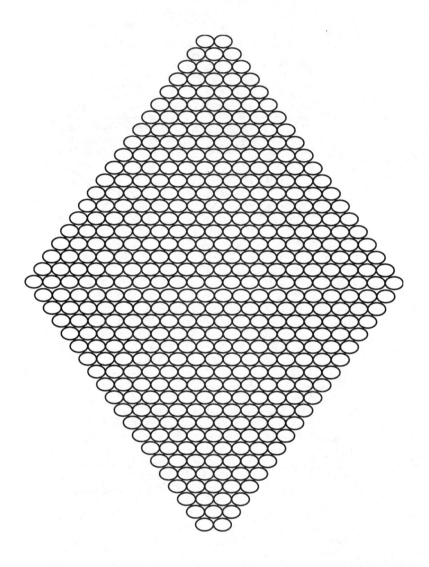

NOTES

NOTES